THE TOTALLY 100% UNOFFICIAL

STEPS

..........Special

£5.99

THE TOTALLY 100% UNOFFICIAL
STEPS
..........Special

© 1999 Grandreams Limited

Written by Joe Adair
Designed by Sue Bartram

Published by Grandreams Limited
435-437 Edgware Road
Little Venice
London W2 1TH

Printed in Belgium

CONTENTS

Who are Steps? And why are we in love with them?

There's no doubt that Steps are magic; a chart-topping single told us as much early on, and with one sell-out tour completed and another in the pipeline, it's no wonder all five Steps have smiles on their faces!

The combination of two boys and three girls that make up Steps is special indeed. Until answering an ad in *The Stage* from a manager hoping to create a group for the new millennium, none of the Steps-to-be had met each other. All, though, came from a world of showbiz wannabes. And now their dream's come true.

So Step lively, put your best foot forward and enter their wonderful world of song and dance!

For a group whose members seem so naturally in tune with each other, it's all the more remarkable that the five Steps were brought together at random through an advert looking for stars in the making. All five thought they lived up to the 'totally talented, totally dedicated' job description, and had the showbiz background to prove it. And, with the Spices high in the charts, there was no need to be embarrassed about being 'manufactured'. If you've got it, why not flaunt it? And they did!

was circling the world as a singer and dancer, having graduated from the well-known Italia Conti stage school. Her former schoolmate Louise Nurding had made it – her time would come too.

What about the boys, then? Lee Latchford-Evans was following a 'serious' career in the theatre, having come within a goalpost's width of taking up professional football. Shakespeare and rock opera were just two of the things to which he turned his versatile hand. Last but

STEPS TO FAME

The fivesome's career to date, from answering the ad to the BRITS and beyond

Claire Richards, youngest of the five, had been a member of a girl group called TSD before answering the ad in *The Stage*. Odd jobs she'd taken while waiting for fame to come knocking included an ice-cream taster – and yes, they paid her! Faye, meanwhile, was puttin' on the Ritz as star of a cabaret band in a swish London hotel – a well-paid job that kept her out of the bed and breakfasts! Lisa Scott-Lee, the most travelled Step,

certainly not least came Ian Watkins, who picked up the nickname 'H' because of his hyperactive style. He was busy entertaining the kiddies at a holiday camp when the call came.

Once the dream team had been assembled, the next step to stardom was to release a single – and with the likes of Aqua and Hanson blowing a very quiet chart scene apart, the decision was made to go with a song that had a dance

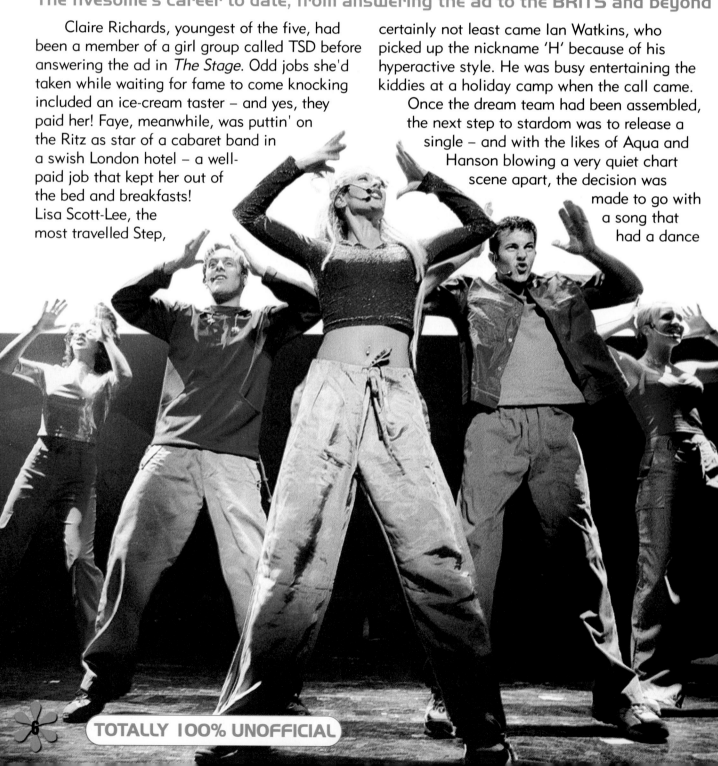

attached. This of course was *5,6,7,8* – a song that tipped its cowboy hat to the line dancing craze that had gripped much of the nation. It was in the charts for several months and hit Number 14 – impressive for a group that hadn't existed six months earlier! The man behind the music was Pete Waterman, the producer who'd notched up over 100 hits for the likes of Kylie Minogue, Jason Donovan and Sonia.

But even Pete Waterman couldn't help Steps promote the record – they had to do that themselves with a tougher-than-tough touring schedule that took in clubs, colleges, concert halls and everything in between! Britain fell in step with Steps very quickly indeed, and when the next single, *Last Thing On My Mind*, was released it shot straight into the Top 10. Steps had arrived! Or at least they thought they had. In reality, they were hoofing it back to London after each show to put the finishing touches to what

would become their first album, 'Step One'. Even then, though, they'd find faithful fans waiting for them at the studio doors, autograph books at the ready and packs of ready-to-drink Ribena in hand. (Ribena, for those who don't indulge, is a blackcurrant drink Steps use to soothe their throats when singing gets too much – they even thanked the makers on the album sleeve!)

Last Thing On My Mind had a really happy sound – not surprising, since the video was shot in sunny Cuba! *One For Sorrow* was an equally uptempo effort, and when released at the end of summer 1998 hit the dizzy heights of Number 2. Like both its predecessors it came complete with its own dance routine, and by printing these on the sleeve of the singles, Steps ensured that fans countrywide were wearing out living-room and bedroom carpets as they and their pals tried to get it right.

Meanwhile, Steps' fame was spreading. In Australia *5,6,7,8* had managed to hit the coveted Number 1 spot, while *Last Thing On My Mind* stayed at the top for ten weeks in Belgium. Darlings Down Under and Big in Belgium – the world was Steps' oyster!

Everything was set for a Christmas hit – and a double-sided one at that. *Heartbeat* was a change of pace, and one of the standout tracks from 'Step One' (of which more in a minute!). But in choosing the 1970s disco hit *Tragedy* to update, Steps not only gave the fans a totally new track, but also returned to the high-energy style for which they were famous. You could say it was the best of both worlds! Take That, 911 and Boyzone were among the other groups to have dipped into the Bee Gees' songbook, but Steps beat all comers hands down with their breathtaking version. Shooting straight into the charts at Number 2, they were unlucky in coming up against Cher and *Believe*, a song that had been four weeks at the top and was set to stay there for another three. But did *Tragedy* go away? No, it did not! And the first chart of 1999 saw Steps proudly atop the listings!

It set the seal on a very happy Christmas for Steps as 'Step One' did almost as well in the album chart. Entering at Number 2 in late September behind the Manic Street Preachers (whose singer James Bradfield admitted his Mum bought Steps!), it hung around the Top 20 for ten weeks before making a second bid for the top spot as Christmas approached. Back up it went from eight to seven to six to three, and though Robbie Williams blocked off the top spot this time, late February saw 'Step One' pass the 1.2 million sales mark in Britain along with four platinum discs for the group members' walls.

It all set things up rather nicely for that month's BRITS, the event of the year to date, where Steps had been hotly tipped to win the Best Newcomers prize. Sadly, the award went to Belle and Sebastian, a little-known Scottish group who, it turned out, had been around a whole lot longer than people realised. There was also a complaint that students on the Internet had allegedly voted many times over, distorting the result and giving the 'gong' to B&S by a matter of a few votes. The newspapers and fans alike demanded a recount, but Steps kept smiling – after all, there'd be many more chances to win prizes. And when *The Times* newspaper says 'Step One' was the best pop album of the year, what did a BRIT mean

one way or the other? And they were proved right when *Better Best Forgotten* blasted into the chart. Once again, they had to settle for second spot, but since they were beaten this time by Boyzone's charity chart-topper *When The Going Gets Tough*, they weren't too worried.

More glitz and glam followed with the MTV Awards in Milan before they blasted off on their first ever tour – a sell-out, natch! Faye was also seen on the TV pop show *Never Mind The Buzzcocks*, but let the side down a bit when she couldn't recognise the lyrics to *Tragedy*! Still, with an arena tour already booked for the autumn (and already fully booked, to quote another TV show title), Steps' life certainly wasn't looking tragic at all!

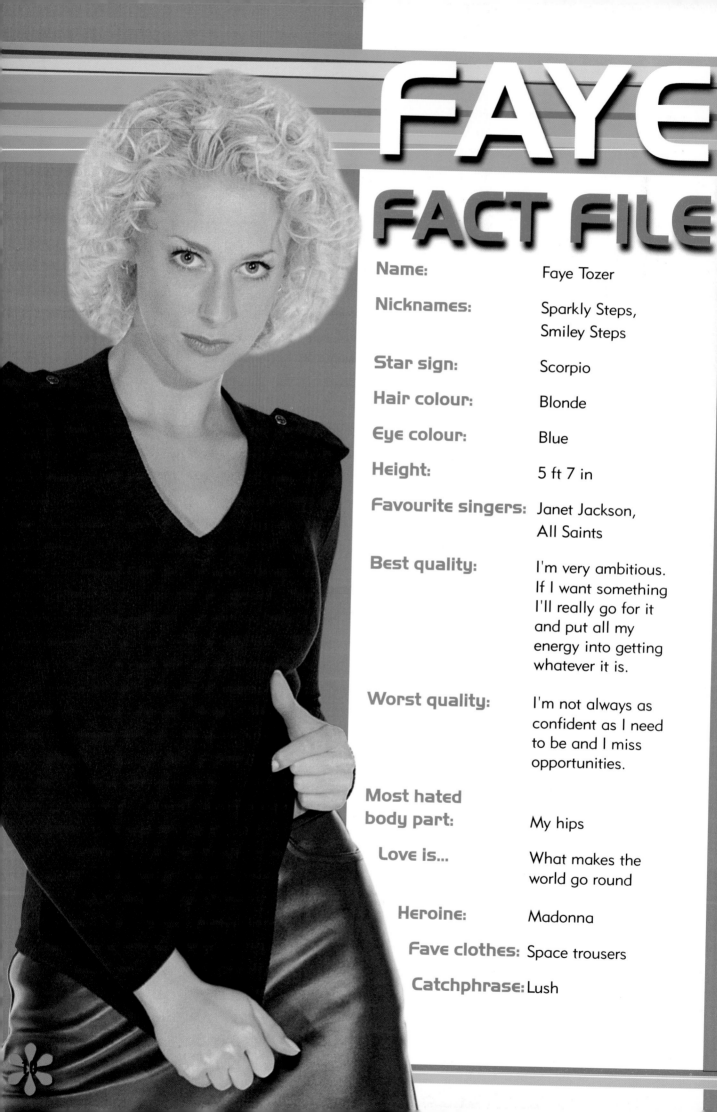

FAYE
FACT FILE

Name: Faye Tozer

Nicknames: Sparkly Steps, Smiley Steps

Star sign: Scorpio

Hair colour: Blonde

Eye colour: Blue

Height: 5 ft 7 in

Favourite singers: Janet Jackson, All Saints

Best quality: I'm very ambitious. If I want something I'll really go for it and put all my energy into getting whatever it is.

Worst quality: I'm not always as confident as I need to be and I miss opportunities.

Most hated body part: My hips

Love is... What makes the world go round

Heroine: Madonna

Fave clothes: Space trousers

Catchphrase: Lush

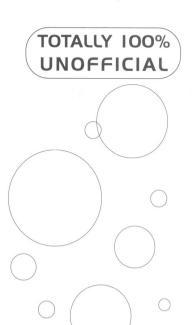

SHINY HAPPY PEOPLE

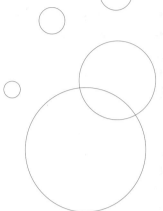

There's no doubt that if you gave an award for the brightest-dressed pop stars then Steps would walk away with it.

Steps have the edge. Maybe it's their theatrical background that does it? Faye certainly took her cue from the stage – *Starlight Express*, to be exact – when she picked the silver and luminous yellow outfit she names as 'My snazziest stage outfit of the year! I just needed roller boots to go with it!' She wore it for *Last Thing On My Mind*, teamed with a silver skirt. Talking of which, the top-most embarrassing thing in Faye's life in 1998 was when her skirt unexpectedly came down during a TV appearance. 'I was lucky,' she admits, 'cos I had a pair of safety shorts on underneath which were the same colour. The skirt came right down and I didn't even notice! One quick step and it was done up again though, so it wasn't too bad.'

What Steps go for on and off stage, and how you can copy their look

It's certain that Faye's the sparkliest member of Steps, easy. She loves gold, and her fave outfit is a pair of gold boots with a gold top and gold bits in her hair. No wonder they call her Sparkly Steps!

The current stage show calls for a whole lot of costume changes, and the fans have certainly taken to the Disney outfits the group have been wearing in the movie medley. We can't see it catching on in the high street shops, though!

Steps' look has become more and more colour co-ordinated lately. Blue is the Colour – so the song goes – and Steps certainly tagged along with that for the cover of their 1999 tour programme. Claire in boob tube, Lisa in T-shirt with see-through arms, and Faye in a saucy single-strap top that must have had the boys gaping.

Most spectacular of all Steps' variations in the fashion stakes was our girl Faye adopting a 'dreadlocks'-style hairdo late in '98. She was wearing this plus a fetching white bride's dress in the *Tragedy* video! Although all female eyes were on the suited and booted boys resplendent in blue (Lee) and purple (H). An answer to every girl's dreams? You betcha!

Photo shoots and record sleeves have rung the changes from red and black (*5,6,7,8*) through all blue (*Last Thing On My Mind*), summery white (*One For Sorrow*) and back to the black and red (*Heartbeat/Tragedy*). Now it's blue again for *Better Best Forgotten*. What next? Maybe they want to keep us guessing!

If you want to copy Steps' look, the first step is to get a nice healthy suntan, because there's always a fair bit of flesh on show. On second thought, check that out with an adult, because too much sun can damage your health. But if Mum and Dad

want to take you to Cuba on holiday, take our advice and say yes! Another best bet is to go for clothes that offer ease of movement, because Steps are an all-singing, all-dancing outfit that don't want to be restricted. So think short sleeves, short skirts and plenty of straps!

The lads are always careful not to outshine the ladies, so male Steps fans may have to make do with T-shirts and combat trousers for now. When it comes to accessories for both sexes, simple gold jewellery seems to be Steps' favourite, often shown to best effect by plunging necklines – but don't choose anything too dangly that'll fly off as you do those dance moves!

When it comes down to it, Steps aren't the kind of group who flaunt designer labels. They're keener on looking good and presenting an image that their fans can afford to copy. These are indeed five shiny, happy people – and so are we!

H

FACT FILE

Name:	Ian Watkins
Nicknames:	H, Hyperactive Steps
Star sign:	Taurus
Hair colour:	Blond
Eye colour:	Blue
Height:	5 ft 8 in
Favourite singer:	Janet Jackson
Best quality:	I don't pretend to be anything I'm not. Lots people try to be really cool when they're not I know I'm not cool. I just like to have a lau
Worst quality:	I'm annoying. I don't know when to stop.
First snog:	I was about 12 and I took a girl in my class the pictures.
Love is...	Fantastic!
Heroine:	Best mate Billie [Piper
Fave clothes:	Jeans
Catchphrase:	Fab!
Secret dream:	I'd like to buy a castle this year. It'll have a b moat and I'll invite all my friends round for parties. (H also has a long-standing ambition to appear on *Blue Pet*

A-Z OF STEPS

From Abba to zoology – sit back and enjoy Steps in alphabetical form!

A has to be for Abba, the group Steps paid tribute to at the BRIT Awards with Bewitched, Billie and Cleopatra!

B means Bananarama – H used to be a fan of the '80s girl group, and they did the original of *Last Thing On My Mind* – or B for Bee Gees, whose *Tragedy* also got 'Borrowed'.

C is for Conga – Steps know all the steps! And Coconut, Claire's favourite Body Shop scent.

D can only mean Dreadlocks – Faye's late-'98 hairstyle shocker – and Disney, their fave cartoons, or Doctor Fox, the Pepsi Chart supremo who loves Steps to death!

16

E is Europe, a continent which quickly succumbed to the many charms of Steps, and Extrovert, something you have to be when performing in front of thousands.

F is the Far East, an area always hungry for British bands that look as good as they sound! Also Football, a big passion of Lee's in particular.

G is for Great Britain, the country Steps proudly call home; Gold Disc (they sold 100,000 albums to get one), and Glam, the 1970s music craze that meant glitter and stack heels. Steps just love to get dressed up!

H means Holland, the home of 1998's Pepsi Pop Show where Steps performed live, and Hits, of which they've got five at last count. Then there's H who is Hyperactive!

I is for International, the kind of fame Steps found in just a few short months. And Ian, H's real name.

J could just stand for Jon Bon Jovi – who Lisa claims to have kissed (in a dream!) – but is more likely to mean Jump, something they often incorporate into those dance routines.

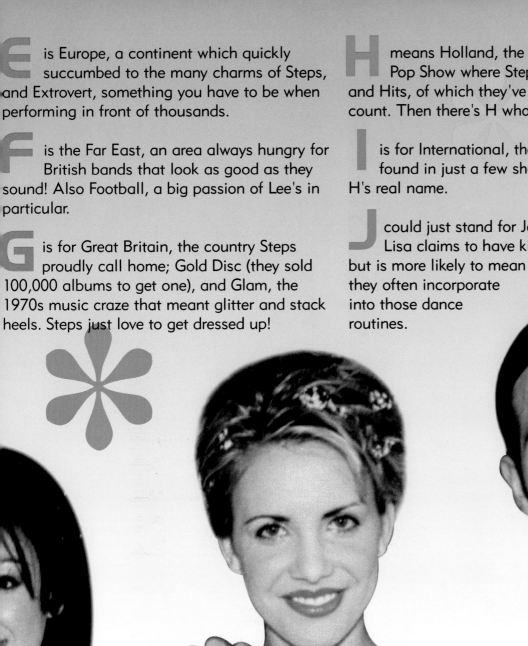

K is the Karaoke Queen, otherwise known as Claire, and Kickin' tunes of course, of which we hope there will be many more! Top tunes, top band!

L as country music fans already know, is Line-dancing – on which the routine for *5,6,7,8* is firmly based. Then there's Lisa and Lee – need we go on?

M in Steps-speak means Malaysia, where a singer went as far as covering *5,6,7,8* in the local dialect. Then there's Millennium, oh, and Music, the reason Steps got together.

N is the National Lottery Draw – Steps appeared on 30 January 1999 – and Naughty but Nice, the label we'd stick on H and Lee (if they'd only stand still!).

O can only mean one thing – *One For Sorrow*, the third single off Steps' brilliant album. But then there's the *O Zone*, a TV show that's always had a good word to say about the famous five.

P is for Party Steps – the nickname Lisa quickly picked up because she loves to party like it's 1999!

Q could mean Quality, which Steps certainly are, or more likely Quality Street, 'cos they're all secret chocaholics!

R stands for Ribena, Steps' favourite fruity drink – H even took a bath in it once! Then there's Routines, the dance steps they take so much trouble to learn.

S means 'Step One', a highly-polished nugget of concentrated brilliance, and Stars – which the five of 'em most certainly are!

T is for *Tragedy* – Steps' Number 2 single that hit the charts in November '98, and Tattoo (Claire has a musical note design).

U – Ah, well, what else but Unbelievable? Sums Steps up, really!

V means Videos, which all five Steps love to make, and Vitality, which they always show in their dance routines.

W is for Workout – Lee's favourite way to smooth away tiredness and stress! And Wonderful, which is the only way to describe their all-action stage show.

X -rated stories about Steps are unheard of! This fab fivesome is squeaky clean, and have even been nicknamed the 'nicest group in pop'!

Y means You, the Steps fans who've made them megastars in record time. Everyone's very grateful!

Z is for the Zoo in Melbourne, Australia, where H got scared by a daddy kangaroo. We hear he's never worn a jumper since!

LISA
FACT FILE

Name: Lisa Scott-Lee

Nickname: Party Steps

Star sign: Scorpio

Hair colour: Brown

Eye colour: Green

Height: 5 ft 3 in

Favourite singers: Robbie Williams, Texas

Best quality: I'm outgoing and confident. If you've got a bit of confidence you can go far in life.

Worst quality: I'm incredibly stubborn and can cut off my nose to spite my face.

Most hated body part: I hate my feet!

First snog: It was behind the school hall with a boy called Stephen when I was 11.

Love is... Only wanting to be with that one special person

Hero: My granddad

Fave clothes: Platform trainers

Catchphrase: Minger! [horrible]

Saucy secret: I like being kissed on my neck. It's quite a sensitive area, but no hickies!

STEPS ON STEPS

What do they really think of each other? Read on and all will be revealed!

'If you want everyone to know something tell H a secret and he'll end up telling the whole world!' **LISA**

'Claire was sick in our room and she didn't clear it up. Then I got up in the middle of the night to go to the loo and trod right in it!' **H**

'In Singapore Lisa and I ducked into the hotel swimming pool for a midnight swim. We got caught by the manager but it was okay.' **FAYE**

'We have silly nicknames for each other that sum us up. Lisa's Party Steps, I'm Sensible Steps as I'm the oldest, Claire is Gadget Steps, Faye is Smiley Steps and H is Hyperactive Steps.' **LEE**

'H and I get on really well because we've got similar mental ages!' **CLAIRE**

'Me and Faye have decided to do a Danny and Sandy (from the *Grease* musical) tour if Steps split up!' **LEE**

'Faye has totally reinvented herself. You should see her passport photo – she used to have really long, curly, dark blonde hair and a bit more puppy fat. She's much more gorgeous now.' **LISA**

'H studied in fine art, so I think he wanted to be an artist. He designed our logo, but it's never been used!' **LEE**

'H is great when you're feeling down, not that we are very often. If you want a good laugh, go to H.' **LISA**

'Claire falls in love the easiest, cause she likes nice things and she's very big-hearted!' **LISA**

TOTALLY 100% UNOFFICIAL

'Lisa dances like Bonnie Langford. I've never done any training, though – I learned to dance at the disco!' **H**

'Lisa goes cross-eyed when she sees a magpie, so it looks like she's seeing two. She's so superstitious she makes up her own rules!' **LEE**

'Faye and I are partners in partying. If I need someone to go out with, then I'll say to Faye, "Come out and be my partner in crime tonight!"' **LISA**

'Claire is the Steps cook. All H can cook is tuna pasta with kidney beans, tuna pasta with sweetcorn, tuna pasta with mayo and tuna pasta with ketchup.' **LISA**

'Lisa and I are both Scorpios, and when we had a day off recently we did exactly the same things in the same places.' **FAYE**

'At a gig H started flicking water at me. I chucked some back and ran out, but I tripped up on a step and flew through the air. Instead of helping me, H tipped the whole bottle of water over my head!' **CLAIRE**

'We all use Claire's stuff. She has all the latest gadgets and make-up.' **FAYE**

'Lee's terrible, he asks everyone for their number. We bumped into Bewitched in a motorway service station, and he said "Don't think I'm being funny or anything, but can I have your numbers and then we can have a chat now and again?"' **CLAIRE**

BEST
FORGOTTEN?

CRINGE ALONG WITH US AS STEPS RECALL SOME FUNNY AND/OR EMBARRASSING MOMENTS ON THE WAY TO FAME

and pushed him into an elevator when they were staying in a hotel in Finland. 'I'd been aggravating them for weeks,' he admits, 'so they stripped me. I had to run around trying to find a tablecloth!' Eeek!

Claire usually enjoys being on TV, but once tripped up some stairs and ended up headbutting a door – with her nose! 'There was a camera crew doing 'behind the scenes' and they were all cracking up,' she grimaces. 'I was going, "Oh-oh, I think it's broken"!' Tut tut – you'd think she'd nose better!

Steps claim they still use public transport – but when they got on a tube train full of schoolgirls, they began to wish they'd brought the limo. 'They recognised us instantly,' recalls Claire, 'and they all came over with their schoolbooks for us to sign.' Little wonder Steps nearly missed their stop – and we'd love to know what the teachers said!

Lisa once fell over in a puddle on stage! 'I fell down so hard on my bum that I thought I'd broken it!' The rest of the group laughed unkindly, but she picked herself up, did a little curtsy and got a cheer from the crowd.

H will never forget, for obvious reasons, when the other Steps stripped him naked

Once Lisa's got her pyjamas on, it's a brave person who tries to get them off (oo-er!). She wears them in cars and even on planes. But even she admits it was going a bit too far when, one day recently, Steps woke up a bit early on their way to their next port of call and she found herself eating breakfast in a Little Chef – still in her jammies! 'Every year this lot buy me

a pair for my birthday,' she explains – so maybe she just didn't want to upset anyone by changing!

H's dancing is a part of the stage act these days – but he can still remember when, as a holiday-camp performer, he had to head up the conga line of happy, boozy holidaymakers. 'I was the leader and had to take the whole group round the camp site,' he admits, face as red as his blazer. Anyone out there got pictures?

When Steps flew to Glasgow to appear on TV's *Fully Booked*, they were waiting for their luggage to appear on the airport conveyor belt when the other Steps decided to pick up H and chuck him on with the cases. 'I was going round and round with the luggage and couldn't get off,' he moans. 'I felt like such an idiot!' Bet he felt dizzy afterwards!

Claire came a cropper at a show when Steps were supposed to be miming. She started singing in a silly way to make the others laugh, not realising that someone at the sound desk had turned her microphone on. 'Everyone in the

except that they weren't in the remote outback at the time – but indoors in a photographic studio! What was worse, the kangaroo meat they were given to cook gave off lots of smoke and set off all the alarms! 'The fire brigade came,' Lisa blushes, 'and I had to explain what we were doing there, in our beach gear, cooking indoors. I felt sooooo stupid!' Look out for her on *Ready Steady Cook* some time soon, then!

H has done so many embarrassing things in his time it takes a lot to make him blush, but he cringes when he recalls the first time he had to appear in a video wearing skimpy swimming trunks (*Last Thing On My Mind*). Never mind, H – we know a lot of fans who'd like to take the plunge with you!

audience heard me singing in this ridiculous voice!' remembers the girl who, just for once, didn't have the last laugh.

F aye ran into a sticky problem when Steps were recording their album 'Step One'. 'I had a really bad cold, she recalls. 'I went into the booth to record my vocals, had a good old sniff and blew my nose, then I heard all this laughter.' What she hadn't realised was that the microphone had picked up the really horrible noise she'd made, and all the producers as well as the group were doubled up with laughter! Maybe this could be a B-side – or maybe not!

W hen Steps were celebrating topping the charts by touring Australia, they were doing a photo shoot and decided to have a barbecue. No problem there,

LEE

FACT FILE

Name:	Lee Latchford-Evans
Nicknames:	Latch, Sensible Steps
Starsign:	Aquarius
Hair colour:	Brown
Eye colour:	Hazel
Height:	5 ft 9 1/2 in
Favourite singer:	Louise
Best quality:	I'm caring and sensitive and I like to look after people. I'm like the big brother of the group – I'm there for the hugs.
Worst quality:	I'm caring – sometimes too caring. It works both ways and sometimes people are like, "Just leave me alone!".
Most hated body part:	The bottom of my legs
Love is...	My first snog was when I was about six.
Hero:	Robbie Williams
Fave clothes:	Jeans
Catchphrase:	Cool
Saucy secret:	I love being kissed all over!

LIVE & KICKING!

The Step One tour 1999 was nothing less than a landmark in pop history. Steps stepped out in big venues for the first time with their hand-picked troupe of dancers to delight their public. If you were there, relive the experience with us – if not, this is what you missed!

The support acts, in order of appearance: Girl singer Lolly was first up, with three happy songs that included her single *Viva La Radio*. In case anyone didn't get the message, she performed in front of five inflatable letters spelling out her name – you read it here first! Then dark-haired hunk Christian Fry bounced on to showcase his forthcoming single *Won't You Stay* – definitely someone to look out for in the future.

By this time, everyone was bursting to see the stars of the show – but we still had A1 to enjoy. A boy band consisting of four highly desirable guys – Ben, Mark, Christian and Paul – they sang three songs. One was their new single *Believe*, a top tune, and another sung unaccompanied, or a cappella – impressive stuff! Yet, good as A1 were, their departure turned the temperature up another few degrees. Because we all knew what was coming next!

THE STEPS SHOW

You'll have heard this on the album – but you'd best believe the tension has become unbearable. After three support acts, it's high time for the stars of the show to make their appearance!

1 BETTER BEST FORGOTTEN
The current single has everyone checking out the dance steps – a kind of double-handed salute, followed by flapping movements of the arms. Do the funky chicken? Egg-sactly! Dancers Lizzy Carlin, Shelina Somani, Graham Lloyd, John Shentall and Darren Cornish are upfront and in the spotlight, sharing the stage with our idols. Lucky people!

2 LAST THING ON MY MIND
A guaranteed crowd-pleaser as the tempo hots up and the girls trade vocal lines on a song which we all know well enough to join in. How are we going to stand the pace? Believe me, that's the last thing on our minds!

3 5,6,7,8

The song that started it all has the audience dancing in the aisles as Britain all of a sudden goes country and western. No cowboy hats, but the girls are using the others as horses – Lisa on H, Claire on Lee and Faye on one of the dancers. Yee-hah!

6 Love U More

Sung by the girls, with help from the blokes, this is a Steps song with a difference. It was first a hit back in 1992 for a little-known group called Sunscreem. Did you know? Do you care? It's so good, neither do we!

4 THIS HEART WILL LOVE AGAIN

Taking the pace down for a ballad that all five Steps contribute to. If you've ever been let down, now's the time to shed a tear – but never fear, the girls are up next with an offer you can't refuse!

5 STAY WITH ME TONIGHT

A duet by Lisa and Faye, both wearing gold outfits – Faye looking especially glam in skirt and matching boob tube. While the two girls sit and sing, a male and female dancer mime out what the characters would probably be doing in the video – clever idea!

7 THE MOVIE MEDLEY: STEPS' OWN TRIBUTE TO DISNEY

ONE JUMP AHEAD

Lee dresses in purple waistcoat and trousers, looking for all the world like Aladdin. The dancers are acting out the characters you see in the marketplace in the film.

PART OF YOUR WORLD

Claire's shimmery skirt and top, which looks as if it's been made from a million sequins, turns her into Ariel, the Little Mermaid.

I JUST CAN'T WAIT TO BE KING

H goes animal with a lion face and fake furry mane – not forgetting a tail that sticks out! He entered with four of the dancers parading in front of him, riding on the other's back. Truly, H is Simba – the Lion King!

COLOURS OF THE WIND

Now it's Faye's turn to shine in a brown mini-dress and a feather in her hair – just like Pocahontas! She belts this out in classic Disney style.

A WHOLE NEW WORLD

Lisa sparkles more than ever here in a gold tiara and purple shimmery costume. Yes, we're back to Aladdin, and she's full of Eastern promise!

CIRCLE OF LIFE

All five Steps take the stage in the costumes that they wore in their individual songs. Dancers perform along the back of the stage on a platform and on the stairs leading up in this Lion King-style furry finale.

8 HERO

A duet by H and Lee, taken from the album, sees them both appropriately in superhero mode. H wears blue trousers and T-shirt with an 'H' on the front in the style of the Superman symbol, while Lee looks splendid in matching purple trousers and T-shirt with a contrasting 'L' in the corner of his breast pocket.

9 I'LL BE THERE FOR YOU

It's time for the girls to join the boys as they romp through the *Friends* TV theme. Claire wears a green top and trousers with a long green overcoat, Lisa a red top and trousers with Faye – Sparkly Steps – in yellow. This was the end of the show proper – but were we going to let them go?

10 HEARTBEAT

It's all white on the night as the band return to the stage to give their all on the ballad from 'Step One' that gave them their first Number 1. Are they going to go off again? No, as we recognise some very well-known chords!

11 ONE FOR SORROW

It's all go from here to the end of the encores – and we reckon anyone who doesn't know the words to this one has come to the wrong concert! But don't leave yet – there's still one treat left to come.

12 TRAGEDY

White was still all right as the band celebrated the other side of the year's (and their) first chart-topper. What other way could a concert so good possibly end? As the lights go up, we're all left with big grins on our faces. Will parents ever understand? Who cares? Steps are the greatest – and what's more they've just proved it 12 times over!

CLAIRE
FACT FILE

Name: Claire Richards

Nicknames: Clarabell, Gadget Steps

Star sign: Leo

Hair colour: Blonde

Eye colour: Green

Height: 5 ft 6 in

Favourite singer: Celine Dion

Best quality: I'm pretty laid-back and I'm very loyal.

Worst quality: Sometimes I'm too easy-going which goes against you because people take advantage.

Most hated body part: My legs

Worst snog: When I was 12 and on holiday in the Canary Islands. He had braces and it was really sloppy and gross!

Love is... Oh, my God! I don't know!

Heroine: Karen Carpenter

Fave clothes: Combats and trainers

Catchphrase: Fantastic!

Secret: My perfect bloke would be someone who's fun, good-looking, makes me laugh and, preferably, has lots of cash!

STEPS SUPER QUIZ

So you think you know everything about pop's most fanciable fivesome? Well, in that case prove it – our fun quiz will sort out the fans from the flops. Just pick the correct answer – a, b or c – for each of the 20 questions and note them down on a piece of paper. No cheating, mind! Then work out your score to see how you rate.

1. What does H stand for?
a) Horrible
b) Hyperactive
c) Hysterical

2. What was the name of Claire's first group?
a) TSD
b) TBA
c) TVP

3. Whose ambition was it to appear on *Blue Peter?*
a) Lee
b) Faye
c) H

4. What's Lee's nickname in the band?
a) Soft Steps
b) Shadow Steps
c) Sensible Steps

5. Who's the Lion King?
a) H
b) Lee
c) Walt Disney

6. Who's the Karaoke Queen?
a) Lisa
b) Claire
c) Faye

7. What perfume does Claire wear?
a) Coconut from the Body Shop
b) Channel No. 5
c) Happy from Clinique

8. Which Step loves space trousers?
a) Lisa
b) H
c) Faye

9. How many albums did Steps sell to get their gold disc?
a) 50,000
b) 100,000
c) 150,000

10. Who has a musical note tattoo concealed about their person?
a) Claire
b) Faye
c) H

16. *5,6,7,8* peaked at what chart position?
a) Number 14
b) Number 10
c) Number 30

17. What did Lee almost become?
a) a professional ice skater
b) a professional footballer
c) a professional ballet dancer

18. What record label are Steps signed to?
a) EMI
b) Virgin
c) Jive

19. Where was the video for *Last Thing On My Mind* filmed?
a) Belgium
b) Philippines
c) Cuba

11. Which group kept 'Step One' off the top of the album charts?
a) Status Quo
b) Boyzone
c) Manic Street Preachers

12. What was Steps' very first single?
a) *Heartbeat*
b) *5,6,7,8*
c) *Last Thing On My Mind*

13. Who asked fellow popsters Bewitched for their phone numbers while at a motorway service station?
a) Lee
b) H
c) Claire

14. How tall is Faye?
a) 5' 3"
b) 5' 6"
c) 5' 7"

15. Before Steps, who was touring as a professional dancer and singer?
a) H
b) Lisa
c) Lee

20. Who is the youngest member of Steps?
a) Lisa
b) Claire
c) Lee

HOW YOU SCORED

1 (FOR SORROW) TO 5,6,7,8!
Oh dear. Are you sure you're a Steps fan? It's time you took another read through this book and did a bit of serious Steps swotting. Then try again!

9-14
We're impressed – but don't go resting on your laurels, 'cos we think that would be a 'Tragedy'! Keep reading, and mistakes will be the last thing on your mind.

15 AND OVER!
What you don't know can be better best forgotten! You're a hero, and Steps will be there for you any time you like!

TOP FIVE

A brief discography

SINGLES

5,6,7,8
Release date: November 1997
Peak position: 14
The line-dancing anthem that put Steps on the music map – even if they didn't all like it at the time!

Last Thing On My Mind
Release date: April 1998
Peak position: 6
Bananarama took this anthem to the charts in 1992 – now Steps give it a pre-millennium gloss.

One For Sorrow
Release date: August 1998
Peak position: 2
The big one – Steps' first Top 3 smash, with a fabulous dance routine to match. Two, too much!

Heartbeat/Tragedy
Release date: November 1998
Peak position: 1
The first Number 1 of 1999, and well deserved. The Bee Gees never sounded – or looked – like this!

Better Best Forgotten
Release date: March 1999
Peak position: 2
Probably the last single off 'Step One', and a great way to sign off – for now, anyway – with five hits out of a possible five.

ALBUM

'Step One'
Release date: September 1998
Peak position: 2
Tracks: Steptro • Last Thing On My Mind • 5,6,7,8 • One for Sorrow • Heartbeat • This Heart Will Love Again • Experienced • Too Weak To Resist • Better Best Forgotten • Back To You • Love U More • Stay With Me
    The album that's sold well over a million copies. If you haven't got it in your collection yet, why not? It's cheaper than buying the singles, and even more fun!

TOTALLY 100% UNOFFICIAL

STEPS OVERSEAS ....
WHAT'S HIT – AND WHERE!

Steps have enjoyed hits all around the world with their happy-go-lucky, danceable sound that jumps language barriers as if they simply weren't there. It didn't matter if you usually say 'funf, sechs, seiben, acht' or 'cinq, six, sept, huit' – Steps sounded every bit as good! Having said that, it was the English-speaking Australians who first took Steps to their collective heart; *5,6,7,8* hit Number 1 and went platinum. *Last Thing On My Mind*, despite stalling at Number 5, also turned platinum.

'Step One' was just as successful. In Sweden, the country where Abba call home, Steps were welcomed to the Top 20 when *5,6,7,8* hit Number 17 and *Heartbeat/Tragedy* went ten places better. In Belgium, one of Europe's smallest countries, *5,6,7,8* sold an amazing 400,000 copies, setting things up nicely for *Last Thing On My Mind* to hit the top – and stay at Number 1 for ten weeks! 'Step

One' went double platinum and made itself at home at the top of the album chart, while the double-sided *Heartbeat/Tragedy* gave Steps yet another Top 10 hit.

India is a huge market for bands, and it was no surprise when 'Step One' went platinum. It followed suit in Indonesia, while in Japan it attained gold status. Elsewhere in the Far Eastern album charts, 'Step One' had become quite a fixture, reaching double platinum in the Philippines and gold in Singapore and Taiwan. But it was New Zealand that really showed itself to be a Steps stronghold: *5,6,7,8* hit Number 2, *Last Thing On My Mind* peaked at Number 15 and 'Step One' picked up yet another platinum album award when it made it to Number 11.

It seemed that wherever you went the name of Steps was a passport to chart success. Forget the World Cup and the Eurovision Song Contest, what they wanted was Steps – providing we were willing to share 'em, of course!

FUTURE
STEPS

WHAT NEXT FOR THE BRIGHTEST HOPES IN THE NEW MILLENNIUM?

It's been an amazing couple of years for H, Faye, Lee, Lisa and Claire – and you can bet the fun isn't over yet!

There are many parts of the globe wanting a part of them, so the latter half of 1999 would be spent touring the world and releasing a new album – 'Step Two', perhaps? Autumn '99 was the scheduled kick-off time for the Steps' Arena Tour – at Glasgow SECC on 24 October. It would then wind through Sheffield, Cardiff, Manchester and Birmingham before ending with an exciting firework flash at Wembley Arena on 5 November. By that time, though, they'd have visited Holland, Belgium, the Far East, America, Canada, China, Germany and Japan (phew!).

The big one was the United States, where even Abba had found it tough going as they tried to duplicate their European success. Steps' big advantage was being on the same label, Jive Records, as Britney Spears and Nick Carter and the Boys. A tour with either (or both!) of them might just unlock the door to Stateside success and riches beyond their wildest dreams.

That was the plan, as Steps continued dancing their way to fame and fortune and picking up many thousands of fans in the process. And by the first BRITS of the new millennium, we could expect them to be in the running for at least a couple of awards. At least that's according to H. 'I'd love us to win Best Boy & Girl Group. That category doesn't exist yet so we'd like to invent it!'

Talking of the hyperactive one, he demands to have the last word. His dream, you see, is to play the last gig of 1999/first gig of 2000 in the Millennium Dome. 'It'd be a special Steps performance,' H gasps, pointing out that three of them live just round the corner so it wouldn't be far to come. See you in the ticket queue!